OVERCOMING BARRIERS

What Is It Like to Be Deaf?

Deborah Kent

Enslow Elementary
an imprint of

Enslow Publishers, Inc.
40 Industrial Road
Box 398
Berkeley Heights, NJ 07922
USA

http://www.enslow.com

Library of Congress Cataloging-in-Publication Data

Kent, Deborah.

What is it like to be deaf? / Deborah Kent.

p. cm. — (Overcoming barriers)

Includes bibliographical references and index.

Summary: "Follows the everyday lives of several Deaf school children, describing what they do in school, how they communicate with both hearing and Deaf relatives and friends, what they do for fun, and what being part of the Deaf community means to them"—Provided by publisher.

ISBN 978-0-7660-3769-4

1. Deaf children—United States—Juvenile literature. 2. American Sign Language—Juvenile literature. 3. Deaf—Means of communication—United States—Juvenile literature. I. Title.

HV2392.K46 2012

362.4'20830973—dc22

2010024709

Future editions:

Paperback ISBN 978-1-4644-0154-1

ePUB ISBN 978-1-4645-1061-8

PDF ISBN 978-1-4646-1061-5

Printed in China

012012 Leo Paper Group, Heshan City, Guangdong, China

10 9 8 7 6 5 4 3 2 1

To Our Readers: We have done our best to make sure all Internet Addresses in this book were active and appropriate when we went to press. However, the author and the publisher have no control over and assume no liability for the material available on those Internet sites or on other Web sites they may link to. Any comments or suggestions can be sent by e-mail to comments@enslow.com or to the address on the back cover.

Every effort has been made to locate all copyright holders of material used in this book. If any errors or omissions have occurred, corrections will be made in future editions of this book.

Photo Credits: © 1999 Artville, LLC, p. 19 (map); © 2011 Photos.com, a division of Getty Images, pp. 19, 23; AP Images: Chris O'Meara, p. 27, The News-Post, Bill Green, p. 33, Richmond Times-Dispatch, Lindy Keast Rodman. p. 38, Victoria Arocho, p. 41; Courtesy of Helene Maram, pp. 4, 21; © Davis Barber/PhotoEdit, p. 6; iStockphoto.com: © Carmen Martínez Banús, p. 13, © Loretta Hostettler, p. 29; © Jeff Greenberg/Alamy, p. 17; Merle Fox Photography, pp. 26, 31, 36; Nicole diMella p. 34; Ross Griff, p. 32; Shutterstock.com, pp. 1, 2, 8, 11, 12, 15, 24.

Cover Photo: Michael Newman/PhotoEdit Inc. (Boy wearing green FM hearing aid sits at a desk with his notebook open in class.)

Contents

Shanel Sigers spends part of her school day in a class for deaf and hard of hearing children and part of her day in her regular classroom.

Chapter 1

Many Signs for "Run"

Shanel Sigers earned straight A's all through sixth grade. She loved to read, and schoolwork was very easy for her. She got bored in most of her classes and wished her schoolwork was more interesting.

At the end of the school year, Shanel's teacher gave her some amazing news. The school had decided to let her skip a grade! Shanel went from sixth to eighth grade, skipping seventh grade all together. She was very excited!

At the age of five, Shanel got sick and lost most of her hearing. She is now completely deaf in her right ear. With her left ear, she can still hear a little bit.

Sign language is a way for people to communicate with others.

Shanel spends part of each school day in a class for deaf and hard of hearing children. She has some of her classes with the hearing children in her school. These are called mainstream classes. In the class for deaf children, the teachers use American Sign Language (ASL). They also teach the students to speak and to lip-read. Shanel knows both ASL and English. By signing, she communicates easily with her teachers and classmates. She has taught some signs to her parents, brothers, and sister.

A Visual Language

American Sign Language (ASL) is a visual language—a language for the eyes. Signs in ASL are formed with the hands. The shape, position, and movement of the hands, as well as facial expressions and body movements, are all very important. ASL is the first language of about half a million people in the United States.

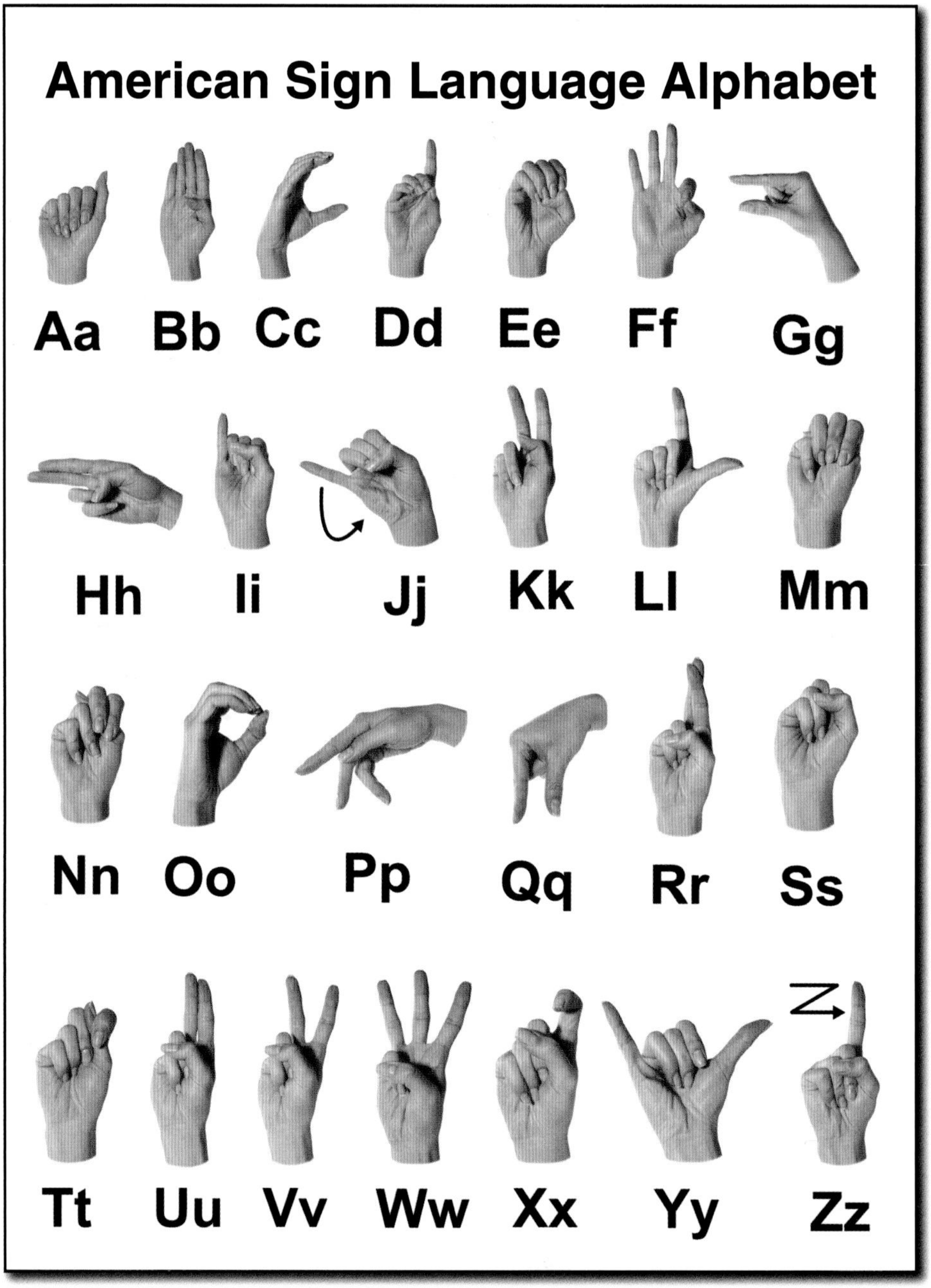

American Sign Language Alphabet

Aa Bb Cc Dd Ee Ff Gg

Hh Ii Jj Kk Ll Mm

Nn Oo Pp Qq Rr Ss

Tt Uu Vv Ww Xx Yy Zz

This chart shows the finger movements for each letter in the American Sign Language alphabet.

ASL has thousands of signs. Shanel learns new signs all the time. She was surprised to find out how many signs are used for the English word RUN. For example, "to run a race" uses one sign, and "to run for office" uses another. A different sign refers to "a run of bad luck," and still another to a "run in baseball." All together, Shanel counted eleven signs for RUN.

When Shanel speaks she cannot hear her own voice clearly. Sometimes she isn't sure she is saying words the right way. She gets help from a speech therapist. A speech therapist is a person trained to help people who have difficulty speaking. The speech therapist helps Shanel practice making sounds that she can no longer hear, such as *p, t,* and *s.*

Chapter 2

The World by Sight

You might think that deaf people live in a world of silence. True, people who are deaf do not hear most sounds. Some do not hear sounds at all. However, a person who was born deaf may not think of the world as a silent place. Having never heard sounds, he or she doesn't feel that sound is missing.

Not all deaf people were born deaf. A person may lose his or her hearing at any age. Some people become deaf due to an illness or accident. Sometimes hearing loss runs in a person's family. When a person becomes deaf later in life, he or she has to get used to life without hearing. The change can be very hard.

A deaf person knows the world through sight, touch, smell, and taste. Sight is the most important sense for people who are deaf. The world is full of color, form, and motion. Deaf people become very good at learning by sight. They pay close attention to everything they see around them.

For deaf and hard of hearing people, sight becomes their most important sense.

People who are very, or profoundly, deaf have little or no hearing. They do not hear a slamming door, a blaring TV, or a fire alarm. Instead, they understand what is going on through their other senses. They know that a door slammed when they feel the room shake. When they see people covering their ears, they know that the TV is too loud. Deaf students see their classmates line up by the door during a fire drill,

Neighborhood street signs can warn drivers to be extra alert. The sign lets the driver know that a deaf child lives nearby. The child may not hear their car approaching.

Some Help to Hear

A hearing aid is a device worn in the ear to help deaf and hard of hearing people hear sounds or words. Hearing aids work by making sounds louder and clearer. Hearing aids are sometimes tiny, but they can be very powerful.

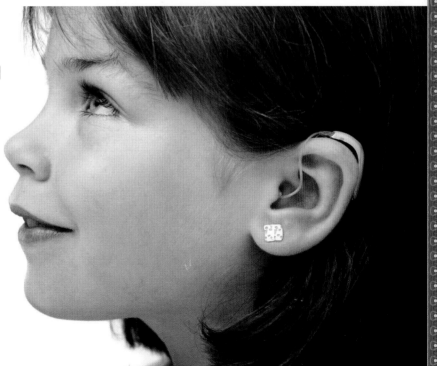

Hearing aids, like the one this girl is wearing, may help some deaf and hard of hearing people hear better.

or they see the strobe light alarm system going off in the middle of class. By watching them and looking at the teacher, they know that there is a fire drill.

Many deaf people can hear some sounds. A person who is hard of hearing may hear very loud sounds, very high sounds, or sounds that are deep in tone. One deaf girl says she has "lawn-mower hearing." She doesn't hear speech, but she can hear loud noises, such as the roar of a lawn mower.

Some hard of hearing people can hear speech. However, they may have trouble understanding what people say. They do not hear all the sounds in words. Sounds such as s, b, p, t, and d are hard to hear.

Not all people with hearing loss think of themselves as deaf. People whose hearing loss is mild are said to be hard of hearing. Someone who is hard of hearing can usually understand most speech, especially if the room is quiet and people speak clearly.

People who are hard of hearing may hear sounds, but it can be hard for them to understand what people are saying.

Sign Language Interpreters

Sign language interpreters (in TUR preh turs) help deaf and hard of hearing people communicate with people who can hear but do not know how to sign. The interpreter speaks everything that the deaf or hard of hearing person says. Then the interpreter signs the words that the hearing person says. Many sign language interpreters are the hearing children of deaf parents.

An interpreter converts speech into sign language at a meeting.

Chapter 3

A Thirst for Learning

Diego Fonseca was born in a farming village in the Mexican state of Jalisco. His family raised corn and had a few cows and pigs. Diego was born deaf. His parents knew that he was eager to learn, and they tried their best to give him opportunities. However, they didn't know anything about teaching a deaf child.

The village where Diego lived had no classes for deaf children. Diego went to the village school, where the teachers taught in Spanish. The school had only two rooms. Children in first through third grade were in one room. Children in fourth through sixth grade were in the other.

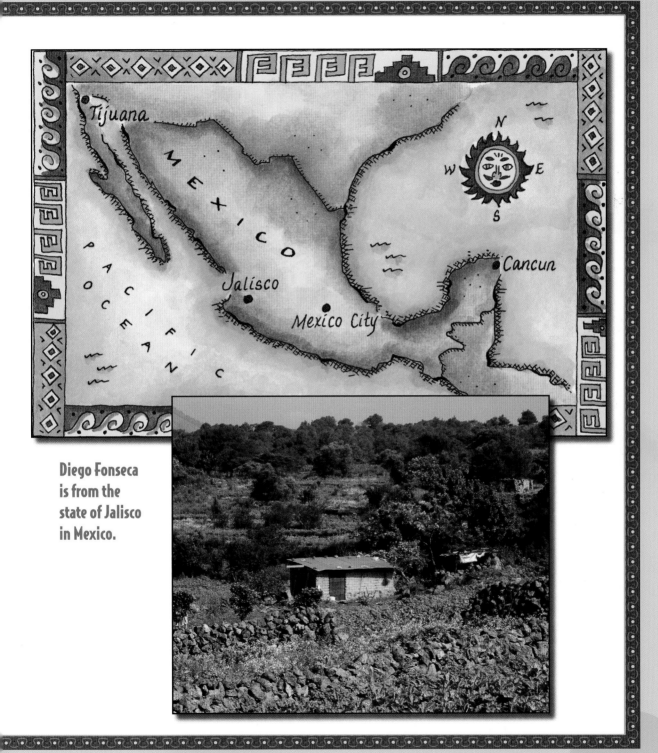

Diego Fonseca is from the state of Jalisco in Mexico.

Diego had a little bit of hearing, and he learned to lip-read in Spanish. Sometimes his teacher explained things to him by drawing pictures. Though the teacher did her best, Diego often couldn't follow what she was saying. It was very hard for him to keep up with the other children in the class.

When Diego was seven years old his parents found out about a class for deaf children in a nearby city. To get there they had to take several buses. Diego only went to school two or three days a week because of the long trip. After two years he told his parents he wanted to go back to the school in the village.

After Diego finished sixth grade his school days seemed to be over. The little two-room school was the only one in the village. Diego was bored and sad. He wanted to learn much more. His parents hoped he could get a good education in the United States. The family moved to Illinois when Diego was thirteen.

Today Diego attends a class for deaf students in a public school. The class is taught in ASL. The students also learn spoken English. Diego learned ASL very

Diego Fonseca loves school, especially his art classes.

quickly. Now he is learning to speak and to lip-read English, too. He wants to be good at three languages: ASL, English, and Spanish.

Diego loves art. He has a talent for painting and is good at making things with his hands. Not long ago he was assigned a project on Christopher Columbus. Diego built a model of Columbus's ship the *Santa Maria*. He made the ship out of wood. It had two wooden decks, sticks for masts, rigging made of strings, and cloth sails.

When he talks about the future, Diego says he wants to be an artist. Maybe he'll paint pictures, draw cartoons, or illustrate books. With his talent, he has lots of possibilities.

Read My Lips

Some deaf and hard of hearing people understand speech by lip-reading. They carefully watch the mouth of a person who is talking. The movements of a person's lips help the deaf person understand some of the words being said. For a person with little or no hearing, lip-reading may be very hard. Good lip-readers use many clues to figure out what people are saying. They watch the speaker's actions and facial expressions. Knowing the topic of the conversation helps them guess words that they can't lip-read.

Lip-reading is a useful skill to have.

This is the sign for the letter *d*.

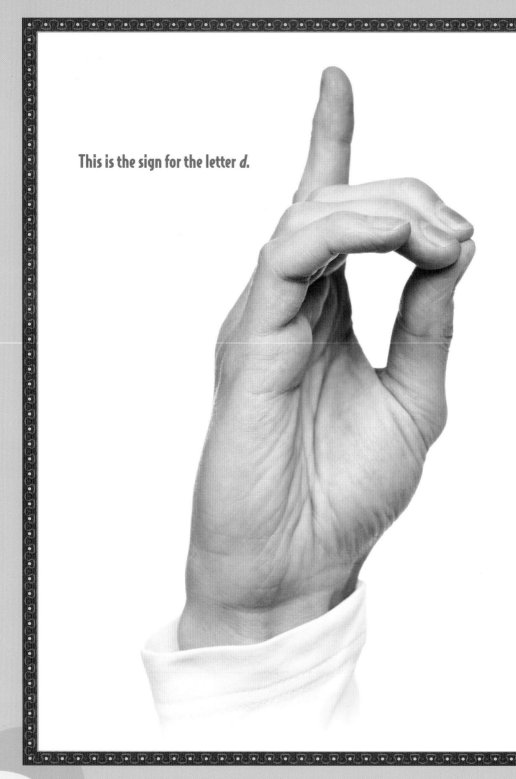

Chapter 4

Proud to Be Deaf

Thomas Gonzalez-Williamson says it's cool to be deaf. He loves to sign with his deaf friends. One of his brothers is deaf, too, and he also has a deaf grandfather.

Thomas's mother is hearing. She learned to sign so she can communicate with the deaf members of the family. Thomas says sometimes it takes her a long time to understand him. She tries hard, and he says she does a good job.

To improve his hearing, Thomas wears hearing aids. He uses his voice when he talks to people who don't sign. When he takes his hearing aids out at night he enjoys the quietness.

When Thomas goes to the library he looks for books about deaf people. He likes to read about deaf

Thomas Gonzalez-Williamson likes using sign language with his family and friends.

athletes, deaf scientists, and other deaf people who became famous. He tries to find adventure stories and fantasies that include deaf characters. By now he has read nearly all of the books about deaf people that are in his school library. He wishes there were many more.

Thomas loves to play soccer with his friends. He also likes to play a game called Hot Potato.

Staying Safe

What happens when the typical smoke alarm goes off? It makes a loud sound, right? But what if a person is deaf or hard of hearing? Smoke detectors are now available that use bright strobe lights to warn people of smoke or fire.

Deaf actress Marlee Matlin signs "The Star Spangled Banner" at Superbowl XLI in 2007.

Bionic Ear

Many deaf children can now get a device called a cochlear implant. The implant is a tiny electronic device that a doctor places beneath the skin behind a person's ear. The person wears a small microphone that sends sound to the device. The device sends the sound to the person's auditory nerve. The auditory nerve is the nerve that carries sound to the brain in order for the person to hear. The cochlear implant is sometimes called a bionic ear.

Players sit in a circle and pass a ball from one person to the next. Each player tries not to get stuck holding the ball when the time is up. Thomas also enjoys going to church. His church has services for deaf people. The preacher signs the sermon. Thomas would like to be a preacher when he grows up.

An interpreter signs the preacher's sermon as he speaks in church.

Chapter 5

Marching All Together

Shavon and Trashauna Tate are twins. They are eleven years old, and both of them are deaf. Many people in their family are deaf or hard of hearing. Their father is hearing and their mother is deaf.

Shavon and Trashauna go to the Illinois School for the Deaf (ISD) in Jacksonville, Illinois. They started going there when they were three years old. ISD is a residential school. Children live there while they study. The school is a second home for most of the students.

In 2009, people in the Illinois government decided that ISD would have to close. They said the state didn't have enough money for the school any longer. Shavon and Trashauna cried when they heard the sad news.

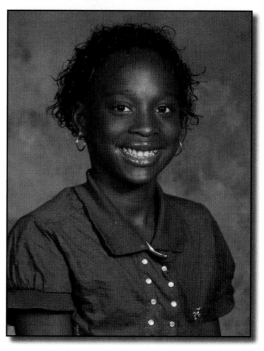

Twins Shavon (left) and Trashauna Tate attend the Illinois School for the Deaf.

They couldn't bear the thought of leaving all their beloved friends and teachers.

The teachers and students at ISD decided to protest. They wanted to tell the governor how much ISD means to them. They organized a march in Springfield, the state capital. Shavon and Trashauna made signs asking the governor to keep the school open. They marched with hundreds of people who supported ISD. They were overjoyed when they

Illinois School for the Deaf

Living at School

About ten percent of the deaf children in the United States attend residential schools. The country's first residential schools for the deaf opened in the 1800s. Today most states have at least one. Students live in dorms and eat in a dining hall or cafeteria. Because they may live together over many years, the students usually make many lifelong friends.

These two students sign to each other at the Maryland School for the Deaf.

learned that their school would stay open after all. By joining the march, they helped save the school they love.

Like most twins, Shavon and Trashauna are very close. They belong to the same Girl Scout troop and sell cookies together. They enjoy the same games

A closed captioned television program has the words typed on the screen so that deaf and hard of hearing people know what is being said.

and movies. They like to watch TV with closed captioning. Closed captioning allows deaf and hard of hearing people to know what is being spoken in a program. In ASL captioning, a sign language interpreter signs the spoken words.

Shavon still isn't sure what she wants to do when she grows up. Trashauna would like to take care of babies in a day care center. She loves helping the younger children at school. She would like to have a job where she can be with little children all day.

Chapter 6

The Joy of Flying

Everyone in Jennida Willoughby's family is deaf. Jennida is deaf. She has a deaf sister and brother, and her parents are deaf, too. When Jennida was three years old, her parents got divorced. She lives with her mother during the week and with her father on the weekends and during the summer.

Jennida and her family love animals. Jennida's mother has a big house with room for lots of pets. There are six dogs and four cats!

When Jennida was five years old, a very scary thing happened.

Jennida Willoughby and her family are deaf. They use ASL to communicate.

Her father and her older sister were in a plane crash. Both of them were badly hurt. Jennida was afraid that they might die. They were in the hospital for a long time. Sometimes Jennida went to visit them. Sometimes she talked to them using ASL through the videophone. Luckily they both got better.

Jennida goes to the Illinois School for the Deaf. Since her mother lives nearby, Jennida is a day student. She lives with her mother instead of living in a dorm. She loves school, especially history, math, and language. She likes reading best of all. Jennida is in an advanced reading class and can read as much as she wants.

When Jennida grows up, she would like to be a pilot. She loves to fly. To Jennida it feels wonderful to sail high above the earth. Looking down at the mountains, rivers, and cities, she sees that the world is wide and beautiful.

This man is using his videophone to have a conversation with a hearing person through an interpreter. This service is called the video relay service, or VRS.

Phone Calls and Videophones

Deaf and hard of hearing people today can use the telephone in many ways. A videophone allows them to communicate directly to each other through sign language via a video screen. A deaf or hard of hearing person can also call a hearing person through a videophone using a video relay service. He or she makes a video call to the interpreter, and the interpreter conveys the ASL message to the hearing person. Then the interpreter signs the hearing person's words to the deaf person.

Chapter 7

Looking Ahead

Shanel Sigers can't wait to start high school. She looks forward to making new friends and taking exciting new classes. She knows that some things about high school will be hard for her. Still, she feels she is ready for the challenge.

Shanel thinks she would like to be a doctor when she grows up. She loves animals, so she might also like to be a veterinarian. Or maybe she'll become an author someday.

In the meantime, Shanel has fun being a teenager. She likes to text with her friends and connect with them on Facebook. She likes to go shopping and roller skating. At home she plays with her dog, a part-German shepherd named Reno.

Pagers, Text Messages, and the Web

Pagers have made a big difference for deaf and hard of hearing people. They can send and get e-mail and text messages from friends and family. They can also get information easily by going online.

Cell phones and pagers allow deaf and hard of hearing people to communicate quickly and easily.

A Love of Writing

When she isn't hanging out with her friends, Shanel likes to write stories. Sometimes a picture gives her a story idea. She imagines what happened before the picture and what will happen next. Things that take place at school also give her ideas. When a new girl joined the class, she and one of Shanel's friends got into a lot of fights. Finally they learned to get along. Shanel wrote about them in a story called "Friendship."

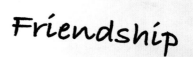

Deaf and hard of hearing people have talents and interests of all kinds. They bring their abilities to whatever they do. Shanel knows she will use her skills and imagination to do work that is interesting and useful in the world.

Hearing people use speech all day long. In a world where spoken language is so important, deaf and hard of hearing people face many challenges. They meet these challenges in a variety of ways. Hearing loss is only one part of who they are. They have likes and dislikes, disappointments, and hopes, just like everyone else.

Words to Know

American Sign Language (ASL)—A language made up of hand shapes, body movements, and facial expressions used by many deaf and hard of hearing people in the United States.

ASL interpreter—A person who interprets from ASL to spoken English and spoken English to ASL.

closed captioning—A system that allows deaf and hard of hearing viewers to read what is being said during a TV show or movie; the words usually appear at the bottom of the screen as white text on a black background.

hard of hearing—Having a small to medium hearing loss.

hearing aid—A device worn by a deaf or hard of hearing person to make sounds louder and clearer.

lip-reading—A way for deaf or hard of hearing people to understand spoken language by watching the movements of the speaker's lips.

residential school—A school that has dormitories where most students live during the school year.

speech therapist—A person trained to help people who have difficulty speaking or who have other communication issues.

Learn More

Books

Ballard, Carol. *How Your Ears Work*. New York: Gareth Stevens, 2011.

Heller, Lora. *Sign Language for Kids: A Fun and Easy Guide to American Sign Language*. New York: Sterling, 2004.

Schaefer, Lola M. *Some Kids Are Deaf*. Mankato, Minn.: Capstone Press, 2008.

Scholastic. *Sign Language: My First 100 Words*. New York: Cartwheel Books, 2008.

Stewart, Sheila. *Listening with Your Eyes: Kids Who Are Deaf and Hard of Hearing*. Broomall, Pa.: Mason Crest, 2011.

Web Sites

Centers for Disease Control and Prevention.
Kids' Quest: Hearing Loss.
<http://www.cdc.gov/ncbddd/kids/hearing.html>

Kids on the Block. *Deafness.*
<http://www.kotb.com/kob2.htg/deaf.htm>

Laurent Clerc National Deaf Education Center at Gallaudet University. *Info to Go.*
The Ear and Hearing for Younger Children.
<http://www.gallaudet.edu/Clerc_Center/
Information_and_Resources/Info_to_Go/
Hearing_Loss_Information/Hearing_Loss_
Younger_Children.html>

Index